DREAMLAND CHRISTMAS LOVE STORY IN 1950S HOLLYWOOD

A 1950S CHRISTMAS ROMANCE OF AMBITION, LOVE, AND BETRAYAL

JAMES HOLLOWAY

CONTENTS

    Epilogue   1
1. The Invitation   5
2. Glitz and Glamour   10
3. The Opportunity   16
4. The Pressure   21
5. Secrets and Shadows   27
6. Between Love and Ambition   34
7. Christmas on Set   40
8. A Hollywood Christmas   46
9. The Breakthrough   53
10. A New Beginning   60

    Afterword   67

EPILOGUE

Hollywood, December 1954

The room was filled with cigarette smoke and the clinking of champagne glasses, the laughter of glamorous strangers bouncing off the walls of the grand estate. Outside, the soft glow of Christmas lights cast long shadows over the perfectly manicured lawns, but inside, everything was polished to a high sheen—beautiful, glittering, and dangerously sharp.

Vivian Gray stood at the edge of it all, watching as the room hummed with a frenetic energy. The Hollywood elite moved through the space like sharks in designer suits and couture gowns, their smiles as dazzling as their jewelry, but as hollow as the empty promises they whispered over cocktails. She had been in the city long enough to know that beneath the glittering surface, this world was more vicious than anyone cared to admit.

She hadn't been invited to this party, not officially. She had slipped in through a side entrance, her heart racing as she pressed herself into the crowd, hoping no one would notice she didn't quite belong. Yet. Her dress was borrowed, a last-minute gift from her roommate, and the pearls around her neck had cost more than a month's rent. But appearances were everything here, and if she was going to survive in Hollywood, she would have to learn to play the part.

As she moved through the throng of glamorous guests, she caught sight of a man standing near the bar, his sharp features softened by the hazy smoke of a freshly lit cigar. **Stan Harrington**. He was one of the most powerful directors in town—known for his holiday films that had become classics, the kind of movies that defined the season. And rumor had it, he was casting his next big Christmas picture.

A role that could change everything for someone like her.

She could feel the opportunity buzzing in the air, a chance to break through the invisible barrier that had kept her on the outskirts of this world for far too long. It was why she had come tonight, after all—to be seen, to make her mark, to prove that she had what it took to stand among these glittering stars.

Vivian watched as Harrington laughed with a group of producers, his voice deep and commanding. She hesitated for a moment, her palms slick with sweat, before she took a steadying breath. This was it. Her chance.

But just as she took a step forward, someone brushed past her, close enough for their perfume to linger in the air. **Evelyn Chase**. She was everything Vivian wasn't—already an established star, dripping in diamonds, and holding court with an ease that only came from knowing you were at the top. Her red lips curved into a knowing smile as she caught Vivian's eye, as if she could read the ambition that simmered beneath her polished exterior.

"Careful, darling," Evelyn said in a low voice, leaning in as she passed. "This town has a way of swallowing girls like you whole."

Vivian stiffened, the words landing like a blow, but she didn't respond. She couldn't afford to show weakness—not here, not tonight.

As Evelyn moved on, disappearing into the crowd, Vivian's resolve hardened. Hollywood might be full of sharks, but she wasn't afraid to swim with them. She had made sacrifices to be here, left everything behind in Ohio to chase a dream that seemed to slip further from her grasp every day. She wasn't about to let someone like Evelyn stand in her way.

Not when she was so close.

Taking a deep breath, Vivian straightened her shoulders and made her way toward Stan Harrington, her heart pounding with the weight of what was at stake. She could feel the eyes of the room on her as she approached, but she kept her gaze steady, her smile confident.

Because in Hollywood, everything was a performance.

And tonight, she was ready for her close-up.

The story begins...

1
THE INVITATION

Vivian Gray stood in front of the vanity mirror in her small, dimly lit apartment, adjusting the delicate rhinestone clip in her hair. The glow from the single bulb above the mirror flickered, casting fleeting shadows across her face. She leaned in closer, dabbing a touch of powder on her cheeks, inspecting her reflection with the intensity of someone who knew that, in Hollywood, perfection wasn't just an option—it was a requirement.

It was December 1955, and the crisp California evening outside felt at odds with the warmth of the holiday season. Christmas decorations adorned every storefront, and yet the air was heavy with something other than holiday cheer. A subtle tension—a reminder that for someone like Vivian, every interaction, every glance, every smile could shape the next stage of her career. And tonight was no exception.

On the vanity table, an invitation lay opened, its gold-embossed lettering gleaming under the lamplight:

You are cordially invited to the Harrington Studios Christmas Gala —December 18th, 1955.

It wasn't just any party. Harrington Studios was one of the most prestigious in town, responsible for films that had defined the era. It was an opportunity. Perhaps **the** opportunity. The rumors had swirled for weeks that Stan Harrington, the studio's legendary director, was on the lookout for the lead actress in his next big picture—a holiday romance titled *Holiday in Dreamland*. Whoever landed the role was sure to become a household name. The question was, would it be Vivian?

She wasn't the only one after it, she knew that much. Los Angeles was teeming with actresses, some already successful, others clawing their way up, just like her. She'd been lucky to get an invitation at all. Her agent had mentioned something about a favor being pulled, though he was annoyingly vague about the details.

Vivian sighed and rose from the chair, smoothing the satin of her midnight blue cocktail dress. The hem shimmered as she moved, a perfect choice for the evening's festivities—a mixture of glamour and restraint, just enough to catch the eye, but not enough to be seen as trying too hard. Every detail mattered.

As she walked to the door, the sound of her heels echoed in the empty apartment. It was modest, far from the grand homes that many of her contemporaries lived in, but it was hers. For now. She'd left her small-town life in Ohio behind years ago, determined to make a name for herself. Since then, there had been bit parts, some decent reviews, and a handful of glossy magazine spreads. But none of it had led to the break she needed. This party, however, could be her turning point.

She paused in the doorway, staring at the small Christmas tree she'd placed in the corner of the room, its needles brittle and sparse. It wasn't much, just a few ornaments and a string of lights that flickered inconsistently, but it was a reminder of simpler times—of holidays spent in her parents' living room, her mother bustling around the kitchen, her father laughing over mugs of hot cocoa. They still sent her letters, but they rarely asked about Hollywood anymore. Maybe they were starting to lose faith.

Vivian pushed the thought aside and stepped into the night. The city greeted her with its usual mix of glamour and grit. Palm trees lined the boulevard, their fronds swaying gently in the evening breeze, while the distant hum of traffic filled the air. The taxi she'd called earlier pulled up to the curb, its headlights slicing through the twilight.

As she slid into the backseat, Vivian couldn't shake the knot of anxiety in her stomach. She wasn't a stranger to big parties—there had been plenty in the past—but this one felt different. There was something at stake tonight, something she couldn't quite put into words but could feel in her bones.

The car glided through the streets of Hollywood, past glittering store windows and the towering facades of iconic movie houses. It was the time of year when the town dressed itself up like a starlet for a magazine cover shoot, every detail meticulously arranged to create the illusion of magic. But beneath it all, the industry buzzed with ambition, secrecy, and fierce competition.

Harrington Studios was a sprawling estate nestled in the hills, its gates adorned with festive wreaths and twinkling lights. As the car pulled up, Vivian caught sight of other guests—dressed to the nines in tuxedos and gowns—stepping out of sleek cars and gliding into the party as if they were royalty. She watched them for a moment, inhaling deeply. This was the life she'd been working for, wasn't it? The lights, the glamour, the fame?

The driver opened her door, and Vivian stepped out, smoothing the fabric of her dress and lifting her chin. The familiar mask slid into place, the one she wore at auditions and parties, the one that projected confidence even when she felt anything but.

Inside, the party was a dazzling display of 1950s opulence. The grand ballroom was draped in gold and red, with enormous chandeliers casting a soft glow over the glittering crowd. Waiters in crisp uniforms weaved through the guests, offering champagne and hors d'oeuvres. A jazz band played softly in the background, and the scent of pine from the towering Christmas tree in the corner mingled with the fragrance of expensive perfume. Everywhere she looked, there were familiar faces—actors and actresses whose names graced the top of marquees, directors who commanded millions, and producers who held the fates of careers in their hands.

Vivian had barely stepped inside when she spotted him: **Stan Harrington**, the legendary director himself. He stood near the fireplace, surrounded by a group of adoring fans, his cigar trailing a thin ribbon of smoke into the air. His white tuxedo jacket gleamed under the lights, and even from across the room, his presence commanded attention.

Her heart skipped a beat. This was it. She needed to make an impression. But before she could take a step forward, a voice spoke behind her.

"You look like you've seen a ghost."

Vivian turned to see **Rob Dalton**, the screenwriter, leaning casually against the bar. He was younger than most of the writers she'd met in Hollywood, with sharp features softened by an easy smile. His eyes, however, held a depth that made her pause—like he knew more than he let on.

She smiled, a practiced yet genuine one. "Just trying to take it all in."

Rob's gaze shifted toward Harrington. "He's a hard man to impress, but I have a feeling you might manage."

"Is that your way of saying I have a shot at this role?" she asked, her tone light, though her stomach churned with anticipation.

Rob gave a small shrug, his eyes twinkling with amusement.

"Let's just say, *Holiday in Dreamland* needs a leading lady who's more than just a pretty face."

Vivian's breath caught. The subtle compliment was wrapped in something more, something that made her both excited and unnerved. Rob had written the script—he knew the character inside and out. Did he think she was right for the part? Or was this just another test?

"Guess we'll see if I have what it takes," she replied, her voice steady despite the uncertainty swirling inside her.

Rob smiled again, but this time there was something in his expression that seemed to hint at a deeper connection between them—one that hadn't fully formed yet, but lingered on the edge of possibility.

"Good luck, Vivian Gray," he said softly, lifting his glass to her. "I have a feeling it's going to be an interesting Christmas."

Vivian watched him walk away, her mind racing. The invitation had been her entry point, but this night was only just beginning.

As she turned back toward the party, the glittering ballroom before her, she couldn't shake the feeling that the real game was just getting started.

And in Hollywood, everything came with a price.

2

GLITZ AND GLAMOUR

The Harrington Studios Christmas Gala was the kind of event that made even Hollywood veterans pause to take in the spectacle. As Vivian Gray entered the grand ballroom, the first thing that struck her was the sheer opulence—glittering chandeliers hung like crystal constellations from the high ceiling, casting a soft, golden glow over the sea of elegant gowns and sharp tuxedos. The room was adorned with towering Christmas trees draped in silver and gold, their ornaments twinkling like stars against the deep red velvet drapes that lined the walls. Even the air smelled of money—champagne, expensive cigars, and the subtle hint of pine from the garlands woven around the banisters.

Vivian allowed herself a moment to absorb the scene, standing at the edge of the crowd. She was used to the lights, the parties, and the small talk, but this evening felt different. This was no ordinary gathering of Hollywood's elite—tonight, her future could be decided. Somewhere in this room was the key to her big break, and she needed to find it. More specifically, find him: **Stan Harrington**.

Her gaze swept across the ballroom, noting the faces she recognized from magazines and silver screens. There was **Evelyn Chase**, draped in a figure-hugging emerald gown, standing near the bar with a group of admirers. Her smile was radiant, her laugh just loud enough to draw attention. As one of the most established actresses in town, Evelyn oozed confidence, the kind that only came from years of being Hollywood's golden girl. And she was, without a doubt, one of the actresses vying for the same role as Vivian. The thought sent a wave of unease through Vivian's chest, but she quickly pushed it aside. Tonight wasn't about intimidation—it was about strategy.

She moved through the crowd, her heels clicking softly against the polished marble floor, making her way toward the heart of the party. Everywhere she looked, people were engaged in conversations that carried a weight of hidden agendas. Deals were being made behind closed smiles and flattering compliments. It was the nature of the business, and Vivian had long accepted that to survive in Hollywood, you had to play the game.

At a distance, she caught sight of **Stan Harrington** again, standing near a grand fireplace, its flickering flames casting shadows that seemed to dance along the walls. He was holding court with a group of executives and producers, laughing loudly at some joke that was lost in the hum of the crowd. The legendary director looked every bit the part, his white tuxedo jacket as crisp as his reputation. Vivian's heart quickened. She knew she couldn't simply walk up to him—no, she had to make an impression.

But before she could strategize her approach, a familiar voice broke her concentration.

"Vivian, darling, there you are!"

Vivian turned to see her agent, **Gloria Scott**, gliding toward her in a striking black dress with a plunging neckline. Gloria was one of the few people in Hollywood who knew how to navigate the business with both charm and ruthlessness. She was sharp, ambitious, and had a network of connections that could make or break careers. Tonight, it seemed she was in her element.

"Gloria, I wasn't sure I'd see you here," Vivian said, greeting her with a kiss on the cheek.

"Oh please, I wouldn't miss this for the world," Gloria replied with a wink. She scanned the crowd quickly, her eyes narrowing slightly as they landed on Evelyn Chase. "I see the competition's here too. How charming."

Vivian followed Gloria's gaze. "Evelyn's always here," she said lightly, though her stomach clenched at the sight of Evelyn laughing easily with the crowd. "I'm not worried."

"Good. You shouldn't be," Gloria said, her tone suddenly serious. "You've got something she doesn't, Viv. She might have the connections, but you've got the raw talent. That's what's going to get you the role." Gloria paused, lowering her voice. "But don't underestimate her. Hollywood's a place where people like Evelyn don't play fair."

Vivian nodded, taking in Gloria's words. She was no stranger to the way the industry worked—flattering smiles often concealed sharp knives. But she also knew that tonight was about more than just outshining Evelyn. It was about proving she belonged at this level, that she had what it took to play the part and more.

"Stan's been watching you," Gloria added, her eyes flicking toward the director. "Now's the time to make your move. And don't worry, I've already planted a few seeds for you. He's heard your name."

Vivian took a deep breath. "Wish me luck."

"You won't need it, darling," Gloria said with a sly smile. "Just remember, confidence is everything."

With that, Gloria disappeared back into the crowd, leaving Vivian alone at the edge of the fray. The moment had arrived.

Vivian straightened her dress and approached the group

surrounding Stan Harrington, her steps slow and deliberate. She made eye contact with the director as she neared, offering a warm, polite smile that she hoped exuded just the right amount of self-assurance without appearing overconfident.

"Vivian Gray, right?" Harrington's deep voice cut through the buzz of the crowd, his sharp eyes landing on her.

Her heart fluttered. "Yes, Mr. Harrington," she replied smoothly, extending her hand. "It's a pleasure to meet you."

"The pleasure's mine," Harrington said, shaking her hand. "I've heard good things about you. Gloria's quite the fan."

Vivian let out a small, practiced laugh. "Gloria's wonderful—she believes in me more than I believe in myself sometimes."

"Well, from what I've seen, you've got a lot of promise," Harrington said, his tone easy but probing. "I've been looking for someone with a unique quality for my next project. *Holiday in Dreamland* requires someone who can be both glamorous and vulnerable. I've seen too much of one or the other in this town."

Vivian felt her pulse quicken. This was it—the opening she needed.

"I'd love the opportunity to show you what I can do," she said, meeting his gaze steadily. "I think I have a lot to offer, and I'm always eager to take on a challenge."

Harrington's eyes twinkled with amusement. "Ambitious. I like that. But ambition's not enough, Miss Gray. This role—if you're going for it—isn't just about looking pretty on screen. It's about connecting with the audience. It's about making them believe in the magic of Christmas again."

Before Vivian could respond, another voice interrupted their exchange.

"I see you've found one of our rising stars, Stan."

Vivian turned to find **Robert "Rob" Dalton**, the screenwriter, approaching the group. His sharp features were softened by a mischievous grin, his eyes twinkling with a secret knowledge that made her both curious and uneasy. He moved with a casual confidence, as if he belonged in every room, yet was above the spectacle that surrounded him.

Rob slid effortlessly into the conversation, his eyes briefly meeting Vivian's before turning to Harrington. "Vivian here could be exactly what you're looking for."

Harrington raised an eyebrow, clearly intrigued. "Is that so?"

Rob nodded, his expression shifting slightly, becoming more serious. "*Holiday in Dreamland* needs someone who can bring warmth and depth to the role. It's not just another glamorous part—there's a lot of heart in this script. I think Vivian could bring that balance."

Vivian's heart skipped. Was Rob Dalton, the screenwriter of the film, vouching for her? His words carried weight, and the way he looked at her made her wonder if he knew something she didn't—about the role, about herself.

Harrington stroked his chin, studying her for a moment longer. "We'll see. I'm holding auditions next week. Make sure you're ready."

Vivian nodded, the words feeling heavier than she expected. "I will be."

As Harrington turned back to his group, Rob lingered by her side, his expression unreadable.

"Thank you," she said softly, glancing up at him. "For what you said."

Rob smiled, though there was something almost cryptic in his expression. "Don't thank me yet. The hard part's still ahead."

"I'm ready," Vivian replied, her voice steady.

He tilted his head, studying her. "Good. Just remember, Hollywood likes to build up its stars—but it likes tearing them down just as much."

With that, he offered her a slight nod and disappeared into

the crowd, leaving Vivian standing amidst the glitz and glamour, the weight of what lay ahead settling in.

This was just the beginning, and for the first time that night, she felt the full gravity of the stakes. Ambition was one thing. But Hollywood was a town built on illusions, and in the glittering lights of the ballroom, Vivian knew she'd have to play the game carefully if she wanted to survive.

And win.

3
THE OPPORTUNITY

The morning after the Harrington Studios Christmas Gala dawned cold and gray—an oddity for Los Angeles in December. The sun was obscured by thick clouds, casting a pallor over the city as if Hollywood itself had woken up with a hangover. Vivian sat at her small kitchen table, nursing a cup of coffee and staring at the phone that refused to ring. The lavish spectacle of last night already felt like a dream, glittering and intangible, leaving only the echo of its promises.

Vivian had done everything right—or at least, she thought she had. She'd smiled, charmed, mingled with the right people. Harrington had seemed interested, even impressed. But the ball was no longer in her court. Now came the waiting, the agonizing uncertainty that gnawed at her every nerve.

Her thoughts drifted back to Rob Dalton. He'd been so cryptic, his words lingering in her mind like the last notes of a haunting melody. *Hollywood likes to build up its stars—but it likes tearing them down just as much.* There was something about the way he'd said it, as if he knew too well what it felt like to be on the brink of success, only to watch it slip through his fingers. He had vouched for her in front of Harrington, and that carried weight. But did he really believe she could do it, or was he just toying with her like so many others in this town?

Her agent, Gloria, had called early that morning to remind her, again, to be ready. "This is it, darling. This is the kind of chance that doesn't come twice," she'd said in her usual breathless way. Gloria had a way of making everything sound like life or death, but in this case, she wasn't wrong. *Holiday in Dreamland* wasn't just another film—it was a potential star-maker.

As Vivian stared at the phone, willing it to ring, it finally buzzed to life. She practically jumped out of her chair, fumbling to answer.

"Hello?" she said, her voice tight with anticipation.

"Vivian Gray?" The voice on the other end was formal, professional. A studio assistant, no doubt.

"This is she."

"Mr. Harrington would like to meet with you at the studio this afternoon. Two o'clock sharp. He'll be discussing the upcoming audition process for *Holiday in Dreamland*."

Vivian's heart raced. "Of course. I'll be there."

The assistant gave her the address, confirming the time once more before hanging up. As soon as the line went dead, Vivian felt a surge of adrenaline. This was it. The opportunity she'd been waiting for. Her mind buzzed with a thousand thoughts—what to wear, how to present herself, what to say—but above all, one question loomed large: was she ready?

By the time Vivian arrived at the Harrington Studios lot that afternoon, the sun had begun to peek through the clouds, bathing the sprawling campus in a warm, golden light. She stepped out of her taxi and took a deep breath, trying to steady her nerves. The lot was alive with activity—actors in costume scurried between sound stages, crew members hustled equipment, and the ever-present hum of filmmaking filled the air. The world behind the camera was chaotic, a sharp contrast to the polished glamour that Hollywood projected to the public.

Vivian made her way through the maze of buildings, following the assistant's directions until she reached the main office. She was ushered inside by a young receptionist who flashed her a nervous smile before leading her down a long hallway. As they walked, Vivian could hear the murmur of voices behind closed doors, the clink of typewriters in motion, the heartbeat of the industry ticking away just beneath the surface.

At the end of the hall, the receptionist stopped in front of a heavy wooden door and knocked softly. The door swung open, revealing a plush office with floor-to-ceiling windows that overlooked the bustling lot. In the center of the room, seated behind a grand mahogany desk, was **Stan Harrington**.

"Vivian," he greeted her with a warm smile. "Come in, come in."

Vivian stepped inside, her palms slick with sweat despite the coolness of the room. Harrington gestured to a chair opposite him, and she sat, trying to maintain an air of confidence, though her heart pounded in her chest.

"I trust you enjoyed the party last night?" Harrington asked, leaning back in his chair, his tone casual but with a sharpness that belied his easy manner.

"It was wonderful," she replied, her voice steady. "Thank you for the invitation."

Harrington smiled, but his gaze was calculating. He leaned forward, folding his hands on the desk. "You know why you're here, don't you?"

Vivian nodded, her throat tight. "*Holiday in Dreamland.*"

"That's right." Harrington's voice was smooth, almost too smooth, like a practiced line. "We're looking for someone to lead the film, someone who can carry the entire story. It's a big role, Vivian. The kind of role that makes or breaks careers. And I don't have to tell you, there's a lot of competition."

"I understand," she said, hoping she sounded more confident than she felt.

Harrington studied her for a moment before continuing. "The character in *Holiday in Dreamland* isn't just your typical glamorous Hollywood star. She's a woman who's experienced real loss, real vulnerability. That's what makes her journey so compelling. And that's what I need to see from you. Something real."

Vivian swallowed hard. Vulnerability. It wasn't the kind of role she was used to. Her previous work had been more about projecting confidence, playing the part of the seductive starlet or the tough, unbreakable woman. But this—this was different.

"I can do that," she said, her voice quieter now, but no less certain.

Harrington raised an eyebrow. "Can you? I'm not looking for just a performance, Vivian. I need you to dig deep. Rob Dalton, the screenwriter—he's written something very personal. This script, this story, it means something to him. It's not just another holiday romance. It's about grief, about love lost and found again. If you want this role, you're going to have to show me that you can bring that kind of depth to the screen."

At the mention of Rob's name, a flicker of something passed through Vivian—curiosity, maybe, or something more. She hadn't realized just how personal this script was to him. But now that she knew, the weight of it settled on her shoulders. This wasn't just about proving herself to Harrington; it was about honoring Rob's vision, his story.

"I'm ready," she said, her voice stronger this time. "I won't let you down."

Harrington gave her a long, considering look. "Good. You'll have a week to prepare for the audition. I want you to come in and read with the other actors we're considering. We'll see if you have what it takes."

Vivian nodded, the enormity of the task before her sinking in. A week. It wasn't much time, but it was all she had. She rose from her chair, ready to make her exit when Harrington spoke again.

"Oh, and one more thing," he added, his tone casual but pointed. "Rob Dalton seems to think you're perfect for the role. That's no small endorsement, considering he wrote the script. I'd take his advice if I were you. He knows what he's talking about."

Vivian smiled, though a strange knot formed in her chest at Harrington's words. Rob believed in her—he thought she could pull it off. But why did it feel like there was more to it than that?

"Thank you, Mr. Harrington," she said, turning to leave.

As she stepped out of the office and into the hallway, her mind was already spinning with thoughts of the audition, of what Rob had said, and of what she would need to do to prove she could bring the character of *Holiday in Dreamland* to life. Vulnerability. Grief. Love.

As she walked across the studio lot, the sun setting behind the sound stages, she felt a strange mixture of excitement and fear. This was her chance, the opportunity she'd been waiting for. But it wasn't just about the role anymore. It was about proving something to herself—that she had more to offer than just the glamorous facade Hollywood loved to project.

And maybe, just maybe, Rob Dalton had seen that in her before she'd seen it in herself.

4
THE PRESSURE

Vivian stood in front of the full-length mirror in her apartment, rehearsing her lines for what felt like the hundredth time. The script for *Holiday in Dreamland* lay open on her bed, the pages worn and creased from constant use. The words on the page were simple enough, but delivering them with the vulnerability and depth the role demanded was proving to be anything but easy.

She repeated the lines again, trying to let the emotion swell from somewhere deep inside her, but all she could hear was her own voice echoing off the walls, rehearsed, distant. No matter how hard she tried, she couldn't seem to access the rawness that Harrington had spoken about. The pressure was mounting, and with the audition just days away, her confidence was starting to waver.

The role was everything. And the more Vivian thought about it, the heavier the weight on her shoulders grew. She wasn't just competing with actresses like Evelyn Chase—who was already making strategic moves behind the scenes—but she was competing with her own self-doubt. This wasn't just about delivering lines or hitting her marks; it was about proving to herself, to the entire industry, that she could be more than just another pretty face.

Her agent, Gloria, had been unrelenting since that meeting with Harrington. Her phone rang constantly with reminders, advice, and the occasional threat disguised as encouragement.

"You need to give everything you've got, Vivian," Gloria had said earlier that morning, her voice sharp over the phone. "This role will make your career. If you blow this, you're done."

"I know," Vivian had replied, a knot forming in her stomach.

Gloria didn't deal in comforting words or soft reassurances. She believed in tough love, and while Vivian appreciated the honesty, today it felt like too much. The truth was, she was terrified of failing, not just because of the role but because of what it would mean for her future in Hollywood. She had sacrificed too much to be here, to be on the verge of something big. But now that she was so close, she could feel it slipping away.

A knock on her door pulled her out of her thoughts. She wasn't expecting anyone. Curious, she crossed the room and opened the door to find **Rob Dalton** standing there, his hands stuffed into the pockets of his jacket, looking slightly out of place against the backdrop of her modest apartment.

"Rob?" she asked, surprised to see him. "What are you doing here?"

He offered her a small, hesitant smile. "I thought I'd stop by. Can I come in?"

Vivian stepped aside, gesturing for him to enter. As he walked in, he glanced around the apartment, his gaze briefly settling on the open script on the bed before he turned to face her.

"I heard you've been rehearsing," he said, his tone casual but with an undercurrent of something more. "How's it going?"

Vivian sighed, closing the door behind her. "Honestly? Not great. I don't know if I'm getting it. I'm trying, but I just... I don't know if it's enough."

Rob studied her for a moment, his expression thoughtful. "It's a tough role," he admitted. "It's not the kind of part you can fake your way through."

"I know that," she said, sitting on the edge of her bed. "But I can't seem to find what I need. Harrington keeps talking about vulnerability, about being real. I thought I knew what that meant, but now... now I'm not so sure."

Rob crossed the room and sat down in the chair by the window. He didn't say anything for a moment, just looked at her as if he was trying to figure something out. Then, finally, he spoke.

"You know, I didn't write *Holiday in Dreamland* just to be another feel-good holiday movie," he said quietly. "It's personal to me. The story, the characters... they come from a place of real pain."

Vivian looked up, surprised by the shift in his tone. Rob had always been charming, even a little enigmatic, but there was something raw in his voice now, something vulnerable that she hadn't seen before.

"It's about loss," Rob continued, his gaze distant as he spoke. "The lead character, Sophie—she's grieving. She's trying to move forward with her life, but she's haunted by what she's lost. That's what the story's really about. It's about hope, sure, but it's also about the weight of the past. That's why it has to be real, Vivian. The audience has to feel that loss, that pain, and believe in the hope that comes afterward."

Vivian sat in silence, absorbing his words. She hadn't realized just how personal the script was to him. But now that he'd said it, everything started to make sense—the depth of emotion in the dialogue, the undercurrent of sorrow that ran through the story like a vein of gold. Rob had poured his heart into this script, and now she was being asked to carry that weight.

"I lost someone," Rob said suddenly, his voice barely above a whisper. "A few years ago. Someone I loved. That's where this story came from."

Vivian's breath caught. She hadn't expected him to open up like this, to reveal something so deeply personal. But now that he had, she felt the weight of his story pressing down on her, making the role feel even more significant.

"I'm sorry," she said softly.

Rob shook his head, a bittersweet smile tugging at the corners of his mouth. "It's not something I talk about much. But when I wrote this script, it was the only way I knew how to process it. To give it meaning. That's why it's so important to me that whoever plays Sophie gets it—really gets it."

Vivian nodded slowly, her heart heavy with understanding. The role wasn't just about her career anymore. It was about honoring the depth of Rob's story, about bringing his pain and hope to life on the screen.

"I'll get it," she said, her voice firmer now. "I won't let you down."

Rob's gaze softened, and for the first time, she saw something in his eyes that wasn't just professional admiration—it was something deeper, something that made her chest tighten.

"I know you won't," he said quietly. "I wouldn't have vouched for you if I didn't believe that."

They sat in silence for a moment, the weight of their conversation hanging in the air between them. Then Rob stood, his expression returning to its usual calm, collected demeanor.

"I should go," he said, glancing toward the door. "But Vivian... don't overthink it. Just be yourself. That's all you need to do."

Vivian watched him leave, his words echoing in her mind long after he was gone. *Be yourself.* It sounded so simple, but in Hollywood, where everyone was always playing a part, it was the hardest thing to do.

The next day, rehearsals began in earnest. Gloria had pulled strings to secure a private studio space for Vivian to practice in, and as she stood in the center of the empty room, the enormity of what was at stake hit her like a tidal wave. Her nerves felt raw, every doubt amplified by the quiet emptiness around her.

She ran through the lines again, this time trying to channel everything Rob had told her. The grief, the vulnerability, the quiet hope that defined Sophie's character. She pictured herself in Sophie's shoes, mourning a loss that weighed on her every action. It was painful to imagine, but she knew it was necessary.

As the week wore on, the pressure intensified. Evelyn Chase's name kept cropping up, whispered in corners by those who knew the industry's inner workings. She was a favorite, after all—a well-established star with the connections to make things happen. And Vivian knew that if she didn't deliver in the audition, Evelyn would swoop in and take the role without a second thought.

Vivian threw herself into rehearsals, barely sleeping, her mind constantly churning with lines, emotions, and the fear of failure. Gloria's calls were a relentless reminder of what was at stake.

But each night, as she lay awake in the dark, her thoughts inevitably drifted back to Rob. His quiet confidence in her, his willingness to share his story, had become her anchor. She was determined not to let him down.

And maybe, just maybe, she wasn't only doing this for her career anymore. Maybe she was doing it for something more—for the chance to be real in a world that so often demanded illusions.

. . .

By the end of the week, she felt something shift inside her. The lines no longer felt like lines—they felt like her own words, her own pain, her own hope. It wasn't perfect, but it was honest.

The audition loomed just ahead, and for the first time, Vivian wasn't scared.

She was ready.

5
SECRETS AND SHADOWS

The day of the audition dawned with a crisp, cloudless sky—an almost mocking contrast to the storm brewing inside Vivian. As she arrived at Harrington Studios, her nerves buzzed with a quiet intensity that seemed to sharpen every sound, every breath. The polished marble floors of the studio's main building gleamed beneath her heels as she walked toward the casting room, her heart pounding in sync with each step.

The waiting room was already filling up with actresses, all of them radiating the same mix of determination and fear. Among them, seated with an air of effortless confidence, was **Evelyn Chase**. She was surrounded by a small group of industry types, effortlessly holding court. Evelyn's bright smile flashed like a weapon, her green eyes cutting through the room, landing briefly on Vivian before returning to her admirers.

Vivian's stomach clenched. There was no denying Evelyn's presence. She was everything the industry adored—gorgeous, seasoned, and ruthlessly ambitious. It was well-known that Evelyn had friends in high places, and her connections alone could secure her the role if Vivian didn't deliver something extraordinary.

Vivian took a seat in the far corner of the room, her script in hand but barely glancing at it. The lines were etched into her mind now. There was nothing left to memorize—only emotion to channel. But the tension that hung in the room made it hard to focus. Conversations buzzed around her, murmured snippets about who had arrived and which names were whispered in studio corridors.

Suddenly, a familiar voice broke the quiet hum. "Vivian, darling."

Vivian looked up to see **Gloria** approaching, her signature bold lipstick in place, a forced brightness in her smile. She sat down beside Vivian, her expression shifting into something more serious as she leaned in close.

"I've been hearing things," Gloria whispered. "Evelyn's been making moves. Harrington's assistant let it slip that she's been talking to the right people. You need to bring your absolute best today, or we could lose this."

Vivian stiffened. "You think she's going to get the role, don't you?"

"I think she's got powerful people backing her," Gloria said, her voice lowering further. "And you don't. Not in the same way. But you have something Evelyn doesn't—real talent. That's why you're here. Harrington wouldn't be interested if he didn't believe you could pull this off. But if you hesitate, if you hold back even a little, Evelyn's going to swoop in and take it."

Vivian swallowed hard, her throat dry. Gloria's bluntness was typical, but today it felt like a punch to the gut. The stakes couldn't be higher.

Gloria patted her arm before standing. "Remember, this is your shot. You've earned it. Don't let anyone—especially Evelyn—convince you otherwise."

With that, Gloria disappeared into the crowd, her words lingering in the air. Vivian tried to focus on her breathing, on calming the storm within her. But it wasn't just Evelyn's presence that haunted her—it was the weight of the role, the pressure to be vulnerable, to expose parts of herself she wasn't sure she could reach.

Be yourself, Rob had said. She clung to that, repeating the words in her mind like a mantra.

It wasn't long before the door to the casting room opened, and an assistant stepped out. "Vivian Gray, we're ready for you."

The words sent a jolt through her, and suddenly everything felt too real. With a steadying breath, she stood and followed the assistant down the long, echoing hallway to the audition room.

Inside, the atmosphere was quieter, more focused. The room was large but unadorned, with just a table and chairs for the casting team and a few scattered lights aimed at the space where she would perform. **Stan Harrington** sat at the center of the table, his sharp eyes watching her as she entered. Beside him was **Rob Dalton**, his face calm but his gaze unreadable. A few other studio executives rounded out the group, their expressions neutral.

"Good to see you, Vivian," Harrington said, offering her a small smile. "Whenever you're ready."

Vivian took her place in the center of the room, the script clutched loosely in her hand, though she barely needed it. The scene she was performing was one of the most pivotal in the film—a moment where the character of Sophie confronts her own grief, admitting for the first time how deeply her loss had shattered her. The lines were few, but the emotion behind them was immense.

Vivian closed her eyes for a brief moment, centering herself.

She could feel Rob's eyes on her, could almost hear his voice reminding her of the personal depth behind the script. This wasn't just a performance—it was his story. His loss.

She began.

The words flowed from her, soft at first, but with a quiet intensity that built as she let the emotion take over. She spoke of loss, of the hollow ache of absence, of trying to hold on to hope when everything seemed lost. But it wasn't just Sophie's pain she was channeling—it was her own fear, her own doubts, her own longing for something real in a world full of illusions.

When the scene ended, the room was silent. For a long moment, no one moved. The weight of what she had just poured into the air lingered, palpable, as if the room itself had absorbed her grief.

Finally, Harrington leaned back in his chair, his expression thoughtful. "Thank you, Vivian. That was… compelling."

Rob, who had remained silent throughout the performance, offered a small nod, his gaze lingering on her longer than anyone else's.

Vivian felt her chest tighten, waiting for the final word. Waiting to see if what she had just given was enough.

"You'll be hearing from us soon," Harrington said at last. His tone was noncommittal, but there was something in his eyes—something Vivian couldn't quite decipher.

She nodded, thanked them, and walked out of the room, her heart still racing. The audition was over, but the uncertainty had only just begun.

The days that followed were an agonizing stretch of time. Vivian could barely sleep, her mind constantly replaying the audition, wondering if she had done enough, if she had shown the vulnerability that Harrington was looking for. Gloria had gone radio silent, which only made Vivian's nerves worse. When Gloria didn't have news, it usually meant things were moving in ways she couldn't control.

And then, as if the universe wasn't finished with her yet, there was **Evelyn**.

Word had gotten back to Vivian that Evelyn was still very much in the running for the role. She had heard whispers around the studio that Evelyn was meeting privately with producers, rubbing elbows with the right people. Evelyn's effortless charm and calculated ambition were working overtime, and it seemed the industry was more than happy to help her along.

But it wasn't just Evelyn's maneuvering that disturbed Vivian—it was what she had learned about **Rob**. Through a few carefully dropped hints from other actors and studio insiders, Vivian uncovered a piece of Rob's past that sent her reeling.

Rob had been involved with a young actress—**Clara Hartley**—who had been blacklisted during the height of the Red Scare. Clara had been a rising star, someone Rob had been close to, perhaps even loved, but her career had been abruptly destroyed by accusations of communist sympathies. The blacklist had wiped her from Hollywood's memory, and in the years since, she had vanished from the industry. The whispers suggested that Rob's involvement with Clara had jeopardized his own career, forcing him to navigate Hollywood politics with even more caution than most.

Vivian's mind raced with the implications. Rob had written *Holiday in Dreamland* from a place of deep loss—but it wasn't just personal grief. It was a story about someone he had cared for, someone who had been erased by a system that chewed up and spit out people without a second thought.

And now, here she was, caught in the very same system. Rob's connection to Clara made everything feel more precarious. If Evelyn—or worse, someone higher up—found out about Rob's past, it could jeopardize everything, not just for him, but for her, too. If his involvement with a blacklisted actress resurfaced, Rob's career, and the entire project, could be at risk.

Vivian couldn't help but wonder: was her growing closeness to Rob another liability? Could it come back to haunt her, just like Clara's past had haunted him?

As the days stretched on, the tension between ambition and personal loyalty gnawed at her. Vivian felt herself being pulled in two directions—her desire for the role, for the success she had dreamed of for so long, was being weighed against her connection to Rob and the secrets that threatened to unravel everything.

And then, one evening, just as the sun began to sink behind the Hollywood Hills, her phone finally rang.

"Vivian," Gloria's voice came through, sharp and clear. "You're still in the running. Harrington's close to making a decision, but... there's more to this than you think."

Vivian's heart raced. "What do you mean?"

"Evelyn's playing dirty," Gloria said, her voice low. "She's been making deals behind the scenes, pulling strings. And there's talk—talk about Rob."

Vivian's breath caught. "What kind of talk?"

Gloria hesitated. "People are starting to ask questions about his past. About his connection to Clara Hartley. It's not public yet, but if someone digs deep enough... you know how this town works, Vivian. One wrong move, and everything unravels."

Vivian sat in stunned silence, the weight of Gloria's words pressing down on her. Everything she had worked for, everything Rob had poured into this project, was suddenly hanging by a thread.

"What do I do?" Vivian whispered.

Gloria's voice was firm. "You fight, darling. You fight like hell."

And with that, the line went dead, leaving Vivian alone with the secrets, the shadows, and the realization that the hardest part of this journey was only just beginning.

6

BETWEEN LOVE AND AMBITION

The days after Gloria's phone call passed in a blur, each moment thick with tension and uncertainty. Vivian moved through them as if she were walking a tightrope, trying to maintain her balance while the weight of secrets and ambition tugged her in different directions. Every whisper she overheard, every sideways glance at the studio, seemed to carry an undertone of suspicion. She couldn't shake the feeling that the ground beneath her was shifting—slowly, but with the threat of a collapse she wasn't sure she could withstand.

But it wasn't just Evelyn's backdoor deals or the murmurings about Rob's past that haunted her. It was the growing knot in her chest whenever she thought about him—**Rob Dalton**. Their connection had deepened over the past few weeks, becoming something more than just professional camaraderie. Their dinners, their late-night conversations, and his quiet, steady belief in her had begun to mean more than Vivian had anticipated.

But in Hollywood, everything came with a price.

Vivian stood at the window of her apartment, staring out at

the city. The sun was setting, casting a golden glow over the hills, and the distant hum of traffic buzzed like a constant reminder of the world outside—fast-paced, relentless, ready to chew up anyone who dared to fall behind.

She was supposed to meet Rob tonight. He had invited her over to his place for dinner, and while she had agreed, part of her was afraid of what the evening might bring. The lines between them had blurred—what had started as two people working together on a project had become something far more complicated. And now, with Evelyn maneuvering behind the scenes and Rob's past hanging over them like a shadow, she wasn't sure what was real anymore.

Later that evening, as she knocked on Rob's door, Vivian felt her pulse quicken. She wasn't just nervous about the audition or about the mounting pressure surrounding *Holiday in Dreamland* —she was nervous about what she might find here, in the quiet space between them.

Rob opened the door with a warm smile, his sharp features softened by the dim light spilling out from the apartment behind him. He looked tired, but there was a warmth in his eyes that always seemed to put her at ease, even when everything else in her world felt like it was spinning out of control.

"Come in," he said, stepping aside to let her enter.

Vivian walked into his modest apartment, a far cry from the sprawling mansions of Hollywood's elite. It was simple, with bookshelves overflowing with novels and scripts, a cluttered desk in the corner, and the faint scent of something roasting in the oven. It felt lived in, real, and for a brief moment, she envied the quietness of it.

"Dinner will be ready in a few minutes," Rob said, walking past her and into the small kitchen. "I thought we could have something simple. I wasn't sure how much you'd feel like eating, with everything going on."

Vivian followed him, leaning against the counter as he busied himself with the meal. She watched him for a moment, her thoughts racing. This man, so guarded and mysterious when they had first met, had become someone she felt she could trust. But was that trust misplaced? Was she allowing herself to get too close, too vulnerable, in a town where everyone used each other for something?

"I've been hearing things," Vivian said suddenly, her voice low.

Rob glanced at her, a flicker of wariness in his eyes. "What kind of things?"

"About Evelyn. About you."

Rob's hands stilled, and he turned to face her, his expression unreadable. "What about me?"

Vivian swallowed, trying to gauge his reaction. "People are talking. About your past. About Clara Hartley."

The name seemed to hang in the air between them like a specter. For a long moment, Rob didn't say anything. He turned back to the stove, stirring the sauce in silence before finally speaking, his voice low and steady.

"I figured it would come up eventually," he said. "Hollywood has a way of digging up the past, doesn't it?"

Vivian didn't respond, waiting for him to say more. She had heard the rumors, but now, here with him, she needed to hear the truth.

"Clara and I..." Rob hesitated, then sighed. "We were close. More than close. We were together. But when the blacklist hit, her career was over. She was accused of having communist sympathies, though it wasn't true. She was destroyed by it, and there was nothing I could do to stop it. I tried to fight for her, but in the end, it wasn't enough. The studio turned its back on her, and eventually, she turned her back on Hollywood."

Vivian's chest tightened as she listened. She had always known that the industry could be cruel, but hearing Rob's story brought it into stark reality. He had loved someone who had been erased by the very world they had both worked so hard to be a part of.

"And now people are whispering about it again," Rob continued, his voice edged with bitterness. "Because Evelyn and her people are desperate to discredit me. They know I vouched for you, and they think if they can cast doubt on me, they can take you down, too."

Vivian felt a rush of anger at the thought of Evelyn manipulating the situation to her advantage. It was exactly what Gloria had warned her about—Hollywood politics at its dirtiest. But this wasn't just about Evelyn anymore. This was about Rob, about the ghosts of his past that were threatening to pull both of them under.

"What do we do?" Vivian asked softly.

Rob turned to face her, his eyes dark with a mixture of regret and resolve. "We keep going. You keep fighting for the role, and I keep fighting for the story. We don't let them win."

Vivian nodded, though her heart ached at the thought of what Rob had been through. And yet, she knew that this fight wasn't just about *Holiday in Dreamland*. It was about something deeper —about the kind of people they both wanted to be in a world that was constantly trying to twist them into something else.

But even as she said the words, doubt crept into her mind. Was she strong enough to resist the pull of ambition? Could she stay true to herself, to Rob, in an industry that demanded sacrifice at every turn? The lines between love and ambition had never felt blurrier.

. . .

After dinner, they sat together on Rob's small couch, the warmth of the meal and the quiet comfort of each other's company settling over them like a soft blanket. For a while, they didn't speak, content to sit in silence, watching the city lights twinkle outside the window.

But as the evening wore on, Vivian knew she couldn't ignore the questions swirling inside her any longer. She had to know where they stood—if what was growing between them was real, or if it was just another Hollywood illusion.

"Rob," she began hesitantly, "do you think we're... using each other?"

He looked at her, surprised by the question. "Using each other? What do you mean?"

Vivian shifted uncomfortably, trying to put her thoughts into words. "I mean, we met because of the film. Because you believed in me for the role. And now, with everything happening, with Evelyn and the rumors about Clara... I just don't know if we're—if I'm—making choices because I want to, or because I need to."

Rob's expression softened, and he reached for her hand, his touch grounding her in the moment. "Vivian, I didn't choose you for the role because I wanted something from you. I chose you because I saw something real in you. Something I hadn't seen in anyone else."

His words washed over her, calming the storm of doubt swirling inside her. But still, the question lingered.

"And us?" she asked quietly. "Is that real?"

Rob's eyes met hers, and for a long moment, he didn't say anything. When he finally spoke, his voice was soft, but certain.

"It's real to me, Vivian. But only you can decide if it's real to you."

Vivian's heart swelled with emotion, torn between the truth in his words and the uncertainty that still gnawed at her. She wanted to believe him, to believe that what they had was real. But in Hollywood, where everything seemed to be a performance, trusting her own feelings was harder than she had ever imagined.

They sat in silence again, the weight of their unspoken fears hanging in the air between them.

In the days that followed, the pressure only mounted. The studio politics grew fiercer, with Evelyn continuing to pull strings and spread rumors. Vivian could feel the walls closing in, the tightrope she had been walking growing thinner with every step.

The film was still hers to lose, but the cost of winning was becoming clearer. If she played the Hollywood game like Evelyn, she might secure the role, but she would lose something far more important—her sense of self, and perhaps her growing connection with Rob.

And as the final decision on the casting loomed, Vivian knew that the choices she made now would define not just her career, but who she was in this glittering, cutthroat world.

She had to decide—between love and ambition, between playing the game and staying true to herself. And in the heart of Hollywood's shimmering illusion, that choice was harder than ever.

7
CHRISTMAS ON SET

The morning air at Harrington Studios was crisp, cool, and filled with the faint scent of pine as Christmas Eve dawned on Hollywood. The lot had been transformed into a winter wonderland—fake snow dusted the streets between sound stages, and garlands of red and gold glittered in the early light. Despite the warmth of the California sun rising over the hills, the festive decorations lent a sense of magic to the day. But for Vivian, the beauty of the scene only deepened the weight pressing down on her.

This was the day. The first test shoot for *Holiday in Dreamland*—and the final hurdle standing between her and the role she had fought so hard for.

As she made her way through the lot toward the set, a sense of unreality washed over her. It wasn't just the artificial snow or the glittering lights that gave the day an almost dreamlike quality—it was the knowledge that everything she had worked for, everything she had sacrificed, was on the line today. By the end of Christmas Eve, the studio would decide whether she or Evelyn Chase would star in *Holiday in Dreamland*.

Vivian had been rehearsing for weeks, pouring every bit of herself into the character of Sophie. The vulnerability, the grief, the hope—she had channeled everything Rob had told her, every piece of herself that she hadn't shown the world before. And yet, the doubt still lingered. Evelyn had continued her behind-the-scenes maneuvers, and despite Gloria's reassurances, Vivian knew that the decision wasn't just about talent. It never was in Hollywood.

As she arrived at the soundstage, the artificial snowfall glistening under the studio lights, she spotted **Rob Dalton** standing near the set, talking quietly with the director, **Stan Harrington**. Rob looked up as she approached, his eyes meeting hers across the set. For a moment, everything else fell away—the nerves, the pressure, the politics. It was just the two of them, sharing a quiet understanding in the midst of the chaos.

Rob walked over to her, his expression unreadable. "You ready?"

Vivian nodded, though her heart was pounding. "As ready as I'll ever be."

He gave her a small smile, though there was tension in his eyes. "You'll be great, Vivian. You've already proven that to me."

There was a vulnerability in his voice that made her pause. Over the past few weeks, Rob had become her anchor in a world that often felt like it was spinning out of control. But there was something different about him today—something guarded, as if he was trying to hold back his own emotions.

"Rob..." she began, but he shook his head, cutting her off gently.

"Don't worry about anything except this moment," he said softly. "Just be Sophie. Everything else will work itself out."

Vivian nodded again, though the unease in her chest grew. She wasn't just nervous about the scene or about Evelyn—she was nervous about what would happen if she succeeded. Would she and Rob still be the same after this? Or would they become just another casualty of Hollywood's relentless pursuit of fame?

Before she could say anything more, Stan Harrington called out, "Vivian! We're ready for you."

Vivian straightened, took a deep breath, and walked toward the set, feeling Rob's gaze on her back as she went. She could feel the weight of the moment pressing down on her, but she pushed it aside, focusing on the scene she was about to shoot.

The set was a perfect replica of a small-town Christmas—twinkling lights strung across rooftops, wreaths hanging in shop windows, and a blanket of faux snow covering the ground. In the center of it all was Sophie's character, a woman who had lost so much but was about to rediscover hope. Vivian had rehearsed this moment so many times, but now, under the harsh lights and the scrutinizing eyes of the crew, it felt different.

As the cameras rolled, she stepped into the role fully. She became Sophie—grieving, vulnerable, yet still holding on to the smallest thread of hope. The lines flowed from her like they were her own words, the emotion raw and real. She could feel the eyes of everyone on set watching her, could feel Harrington and Rob's silent appraisal. But she didn't care. In that moment, it was just her and Sophie's story, the story that Rob had entrusted to her.

The pivotal moment of the scene arrived—a quiet, heartbreaking admission of loss, followed by a spark of hope. Vivian felt the emotion swell in her chest, her voice catching as she delivered the line that Rob had written with such care. She could hear the tremor in her voice, could feel the tears welling in her eyes, but she didn't hold back. She let it all out.

When the scene ended, there was a moment of silence on set. The quiet stretched, as if everyone was holding their breath. Then, Harrington nodded, his expression inscrutable, but there was something approving in the way he looked at her.

"Good," he said simply. "Let's break for now. We'll be back after lunch."

Vivian let out a breath she hadn't realized she was holding. The scene was done, but the decision was far from made. She glanced over at Rob, who stood at the edge of the set, his eyes locked on hers. He gave her a small nod, but there was a tightness in his expression that sent a ripple of unease through her.

Later that afternoon, as the crew broke for the holidays, the studio fell into an almost eerie quiet. The once-bustling set was now empty, the fake snow and twinkling lights feeling hollow in the absence of the usual hustle and bustle.

Vivian lingered, unsure of where to go, unsure of what came next. She had given everything to the role, but was it enough? And if it wasn't, what would she do?

She found herself wandering back toward the now-quiet set, the quiet enveloping her like a blanket. The Christmas decorations glittered in the fading light, and the air was still. The moment felt surreal, as if the world was holding its breath, waiting for something to break the silence.

"Vivian."

She turned to find **Evelyn Chase** standing behind her, her emerald dress a stark contrast against the wintery set. Evelyn's expression was calm, but there was a sharpness in her eyes that made Vivian's skin prickle.

"You did well today," Evelyn said, her voice smooth, but with an undertone that made Vivian wary. "I can see why Rob believes in you."

Vivian didn't respond, unsure of where this conversation was headed. She had learned long ago that Evelyn never said anything without a reason.

"But you should know something, Vivian," Evelyn continued,

stepping closer. "Belief doesn't always win in Hollywood. Power does. Connections. And I have those."

Vivian clenched her jaw, the tension that had been building all day rising to the surface. "What are you saying, Evelyn?"

Evelyn's smile was cold. "I'm saying that while you were busy trying to impress the director with your talent, I've been making sure the people who matter know who I am. Harrington may like you, but this decision isn't just his to make. And if it comes down to connections, well... you know how this works."

Vivian's heart raced, anger flaring in her chest. She had fought so hard, had poured every bit of herself into this role, and now Evelyn was telling her it might not matter? That no matter how good she was, Hollywood's game might still be rigged against her?

"You can't control everything, Evelyn," Vivian said, her voice steady despite the anger bubbling underneath. "Not this time."

Evelyn's smile faltered for a brief second, then she stepped back, her expression cool and composed. "We'll see," she said lightly. "But don't say I didn't warn you."

With that, Evelyn turned and walked away, leaving Vivian standing alone in the empty set, the Christmas lights twinkling above her like false promises.

That evening, as the crew gathered for a final holiday party at the studio, Vivian found herself once again caught between the glittering facade of Hollywood and the reality of what she was up against. The room was filled with laughter, champagne glasses clinking, and festive music playing in the background. But beneath the surface, everyone was waiting—waiting for the final decision, waiting to see who would win the role of Sophie.

Vivian stood by the window, looking out at the glittering city below. The decision would come tomorrow—Christmas Day. The studio would announce the final casting, and her future would be decided.

She heard footsteps behind her and turned to see Rob approaching, his expression unreadable.

"You were amazing today," he said quietly.

Vivian smiled faintly, though the tension in her chest remained. "Thank you. I just hope it was enough."

Rob hesitated, then stepped closer, his voice low. "It was. I believe in you, Vivian. But no matter what happens tomorrow… don't forget who you are. Don't let this place change you."

Vivian's heart ached at his words, at the quiet desperation in his voice. She wanted to tell him that she wouldn't, that she could stay true to herself in a town that demanded so much. But the truth was, she wasn't sure anymore. Hollywood had a way of taking what you were and molding it into something else—something shinier, more glamorous, but less real.

"I won't," she whispered, though the words felt heavy on her tongue.

As the party continued around them, the glittering lights reflecting off the champagne glasses, Vivian felt the weight of tomorrow pressing down on her. She had fought for this moment, for this role, but now that it was within reach, she wasn't sure if she could grasp it without losing herself in the process.

And as she stood beside Rob, their future hanging in the balance, she realized that this wasn't just a test of her talent. It was a test of who she was—and who she wanted to become.

Tomorrow, the studio would make their decision. But tonight, on the eve of Christmas, Vivian found herself standing at the crossroads of ambition, love, and self-worth.

And in Hollywood, where everything glittered but nothing was as it seemed, she wasn't sure which path she would choose.

8

A HOLLYWOOD CHRISTMAS

Christmas Day in Hollywood arrived with a rare chill in the air, the sharp winter sun casting long shadows over the palm-lined streets. Despite the festive decorations that adorned the city, the morning felt tense, brimming with anticipation for what the day would bring. For most people, Christmas meant family gatherings, gift exchanges, and holiday cheer. But for Vivian, today was about something far less comforting: the final decision.

The night before had felt like a blur—a haze of Christmas lights, glittering faces, and champagne. Rob's words still echoed in her mind: *Don't let this place change you.* But it was hard to know how much of herself she had already lost to the industry. The game had become everything—the ambition, the fight for the role, and, somewhere in the middle of it all, the fragile connection she had built with Rob. Now, as she stood on the precipice of success or failure, she wondered if she could ever separate the two again.

Vivian sat in front of the vanity in her apartment, staring at her reflection. The girl who had left Ohio full of dreams and fire felt distant, almost like a character she used to play. In her place was someone harder, someone who had learned the art of Hollywood survival. But beneath the polished exterior, she could still feel the cracks—the vulnerability Rob had urged her to embrace for the role, the part of her that wasn't sure if she was ready to win or lose today.

The phone rang, its sharp sound cutting through the quiet of the morning. Vivian's heart leaped into her throat as she reached for it, her fingers trembling slightly.

"Hello?"

"Vivian, darling," came **Gloria's** familiar voice, smooth but tinged with tension. "Merry Christmas."

"Merry Christmas," Vivian replied, her voice steady despite the rising anxiety in her chest. She didn't need to ask why Gloria was calling. This was the moment.

"I've just spoken to Harrington," Gloria continued, her voice careful. "The studio has made their decision."

Vivian held her breath, waiting for the words that would either change her life or crush everything she had been working toward.

"They've chosen you, Vivian," Gloria said finally, her voice warm with pride. "You've got the role."

Vivian felt the world tilt beneath her. For a moment, she couldn't speak, couldn't move, couldn't breathe. She had done it. She had won.

"I... I got the role?" she repeated, as if needing to hear the words again to believe them.

"You did, darling," Gloria confirmed. "Stan was impressed. The test shoot sealed it for him. You brought something to Sophie that no one else could. Even Evelyn couldn't argue with that."

Vivian exhaled, the tension in her chest releasing in a wave. She had done it. She had succeeded. All the pressure, all the fear, all the sacrifices—this was the moment she had been fighting for.

But as the realization sank in, it wasn't the surge of joy she had expected. Instead, a strange emptiness settled inside her.

Gloria's voice cut through her thoughts. "This is your big break, Vivian. The real start of your career. But there's more to it. I need you to be smart about this. Now that you've won the role, the studio is going to watch you closely. Harrington might have picked you, but you'll have to navigate the politics carefully. Evelyn's still around, and she's not going to forget this. Understand?"

Vivian nodded, though Gloria couldn't see her. "I understand."

"Good," Gloria said, her voice softening. "This is a big win, Vivian. Enjoy it. You've earned it."

After a few more pleasantries, Gloria hung up, leaving Vivian alone with the news that should have been the best gift she'd ever received.

But as she sat there, staring at the phone, the elation she had expected never fully arrived. Winning the role hadn't brought the sense of triumph she'd dreamed of. Instead, it left her questioning everything—the price she had paid, the parts of herself she had given up along the way.

By late afternoon, Vivian found herself at the Harrington Studios Christmas party. The studio had spared no expense in making the day feel magical. The lot was transformed into a holiday paradise, with artificial snow falling gently over twinkling lights, a massive Christmas tree towering in the center of the courtyard, and music drifting through the air like a scene out of a movie.

Vivian moved through the crowd, accepting congratulations from actors and producers, casting directors and studio executives. Everyone seemed to know she had won the role—her victory was the talk of the party. But with each passing smile, with each glass of champagne raised in her honor, the sense of hollowness inside her only grew.

She spotted **Evelyn Chase** across the courtyard, standing with a group of producers, her green dress shimmering in the evening light. Evelyn's face was a mask of practiced poise, but there was no denying the simmering resentment in her eyes when they briefly met Vivian's.

Evelyn had lost this round, but she wasn't out of the game. Vivian knew that much. In Hollywood, there were always more roles, more power plays, more opportunities for those who refused to stay down. Evelyn would recover. She always did.

"Congratulations, Vivian," a voice said behind her, pulling her from her thoughts.

Vivian turned to see **Stan Harrington** approaching, a glass of whiskey in his hand and a satisfied smile on his face.

"Thank you," Vivian replied, offering him a small smile of her own.

"You earned it," Harrington said, his voice warm but matter-of-fact. "Your audition was the best I've seen in a long time. Sophie needs someone with depth, someone who can carry the weight of the story. You're that person."

Vivian nodded, though the words felt heavy in her chest. "I appreciate that, Mr. Harrington."

He studied her for a moment, his gaze thoughtful. "This is just the beginning, you know. This role will change everything for you. But you'll have to be smart about it. Hollywood is a fickle place. Stay grounded."

Vivian met his eyes, unsure of how to respond. Was it even possible to stay grounded in a world that seemed determined to mold her into something else?

Harrington raised his glass. "Here's to your success, Vivian. Merry Christmas."

"Merry Christmas," she echoed, watching as he drifted back

into the crowd, already lost among the glittering faces and whispered conversations.

As the night wore on, the party grew louder, more celebratory, but Vivian felt increasingly distant from it all. The role was hers—*Holiday in Dreamland* was her big break—but the excitement she had once imagined felt strangely out of reach.

She moved to the edge of the courtyard, seeking a moment of quiet away from the crowd. The Christmas lights glittered above her, casting a soft glow over the lot, but the festive atmosphere only made the hollowness inside her more acute. She had wanted this for so long, had worked and sacrificed for it. So why did it feel so empty?

"Vivian."

She turned to see **Rob Dalton** standing just a few feet away, his expression unreadable. He hadn't approached her all evening, and part of her had wondered if he was avoiding her. But now, here he was, standing in the quiet between the lights and shadows, and the weight of everything that had passed between them seemed to hang in the air.

"You did it," he said softly, his voice carrying a mix of pride and something else—something heavier, something unspoken.

"I did," she replied, though her voice lacked the joy she had expected.

Rob stepped closer, his eyes searching hers. "I saw you at the party. You don't seem... happy."

Vivian looked away, staring at the twinkling lights above them. "I thought winning the role would feel different. I thought it would mean more."

Rob was silent for a moment, then spoke softly. "Hollywood has a way of making us believe that winning is everything. But it's not."

Vivian turned to him, her chest tight. "Then what is?"

Rob's eyes held hers, his expression serious. "It's the people we become in the process. It's the relationships we build, the parts of ourselves we hold on to, even when the industry tries to take them away."

Vivian felt the words sink in, cutting through the glittering facade of the night. She had won the role, but at what cost? Had she lost parts of herself along the way? Had her ambition pushed her too far from the person she had once been?

"I don't know who I am anymore," she admitted, her voice barely a whisper.

Rob's expression softened, and he stepped closer, reaching for her hand. "You're still you, Vivian. You've always been you. But Hollywood... it can make us forget that."

For a moment, they stood in silence, the distance between them closing as Rob held her hand, grounding her in the moment. The lights around them shimmered, but the world felt quieter, more real.

"What happens now?" Vivian asked, her voice trembling slightly.

Rob met her gaze, his eyes filled with a mixture of hope and uncertainty. "That's up to you."

As the night deepened and the party began to wind down, Vivian and Rob found themselves alone beneath the Christmas lights, the noise of the world fading into the background. The role was hers. But more importantly, she realized, her future was hers to decide.

Hollywood had offered her everything she had once dreamed of, but in the end, it had also shown her the cost of chasing that dream. Ambition had brought her to this moment, but it was love

—love for her craft, for Rob, for herself—that would carry her forward.

And as the lights of Hollywood twinkled above them like stars in the sky, Vivian knew that whatever came next, she was ready to face it—not as the person Hollywood wanted her to be, but as the person she had always been.

In the quiet of that magical Hollywood Christmas night, Vivian Gray stood at the crossroads of her ambition and her heart, finally understanding that the real gift she had received was the one she had been searching for all along—herself.

9
THE BREAKTHROUGH

The morning of the first official day of shooting *Holiday in Dreamland* was electric with energy. The buzz of activity on the Harrington Studios lot was palpable—crews moving equipment, assistants rushing with last-minute notes, and actors slipping into costumes, their faces a mixture of nerves and excitement. It felt like the start of something monumental, and Vivian could sense it in the air. This was her moment, the one she had fought so hard for, and she knew the whole world would be watching.

As she arrived on set, dressed in the simple, elegant costume of her character Sophie, a wave of nervous excitement surged through her. The set, an idyllic Christmas town draped in shimmering lights and snowy streets, stood before her, ready to be transformed into the magical world that Rob had crafted in his script. It was the kind of dreamlike setting that made her feel as though she had stepped into a storybook.

But beneath the glitz and holiday cheer, the tension was undeniable. **Evelyn Chase** might have lost the role, but she was still part of the project—cast as a supporting character, much to her visible dismay. She had been gracious in front of the press, congratulating Vivian with a dazzling smile, but there was an edge to her now, a quiet intensity that made Vivian uneasy. Evelyn was too seasoned, too calculating, to let a single defeat derail her. And that knowledge sat in the back of Vivian's mind like a quiet warning.

Vivian made her way through the set, offering small smiles to crew members as she passed. She knew what was expected of her today—this wasn't just about delivering a good performance. It was about proving that Harrington had made the right choice. The entire cast and crew, not to mention the Hollywood press, were waiting to see if she could live up to the hype.

She spotted **Rob Dalton** near one of the camera setups, talking quietly with **Stan Harrington**. Rob's eyes found hers across the bustling set, and a subtle smile tugged at his lips. It was a brief, quiet moment between them—one that grounded her in the chaos. His presence, his belief in her, had become her anchor, and she clung to that now.

Vivian moved toward them, her heart pounding with anticipation. She had been rehearsing for weeks, but nothing compared to the adrenaline of shooting the first scene. This was it. This was real.

"Vivian," Harrington said, his sharp eyes assessing her as she approached. "Ready to start?"

Vivian nodded, her stomach tight with nerves but her resolve firm. "Ready."

Harrington looked pleased, though his expression remained as focused as ever. "We'll start with the scene where Sophie sees the Christmas tree in the town square for the first time—the moment where she begins to feel hope again. It's a subtle one, but important. Make sure to show the shift in her. She's not broken, not anymore. She's finding her way back."

Vivian nodded, absorbing his direction. This was the core of the film—the transformation of Sophie from grief to hope, from loss to love. She understood the weight of it, not just in terms of the script but in terms of Rob's own story. This scene, this moment, was personal for him.

Rob stepped forward, his eyes filled with the same intensity she had seen the night they first talked about the script's meaning. "Don't overthink it," he said softly. "Just feel it. You know this character. You know what she's been through."

Vivian met his gaze, her pulse quickening. He was right. She had lived with Sophie's emotions for weeks, let them intertwine with her own fears and hopes. She could do this. She would do this.

The crew began to set up for the scene, adjusting lights and cameras. The set, an enchanted village square adorned with twinkling Christmas lights and a massive tree at its center, looked breathtaking under the studio's careful design. Vivian positioned herself at the start mark, ready to walk into the scene where Sophie's heart begins to heal. The air was charged with tension, every eye on her.

"Quiet on set!" the assistant director called out. "And... action!"

The world narrowed to the sound of the director's voice, the faint hum of the cameras rolling, and the delicate snowfall drifting around her. Vivian stepped forward, her footsteps slow and deliberate, her breath catching in her throat as she approached the towering Christmas tree that symbolized so much more than holiday cheer. It symbolized renewal. Hope. The possibility of love after loss.

The emotions swelled in her chest as she looked up at the tree, her eyes reflecting the soft glow of the lights. She felt Sophie's grief, her lingering pain—but also, for the first time, she allowed herself to feel the hope that Rob had written into the script. She let it fill her, let it seep into her expression. She didn't have to force it; the emotions were real, raw, just beneath the surface.

She heard the faint sound of carolers in the background, their voices a haunting reminder of the holiday's bittersweet beauty. In that moment, it wasn't just Sophie who was beginning to heal—it was Vivian, too. The lines between them blurred, and the weight of what she had fought for, both in her career and in her personal life, settled around her like the falling snow.

The scene unfolded quietly, beautifully, as she let Sophie's emotions play out with every glance, every breath. And when the camera finally pulled away, signaling the end of the take, the set fell into a charged silence.

"Cut!" Harrington's voice broke through the stillness. "That's it. Perfect."

Vivian exhaled slowly, her chest tight with the aftershocks of emotion. She had done it. She had brought Sophie to life, and she could feel in the air that everyone around her had felt it, too. The crew clapped, and Harrington gave her a rare, approving smile.

But before she could fully take in the moment, there was a sudden ripple of movement on set. A small group of people had gathered at the edge of the lot, their attention focused not on her performance, but on a heated conversation happening just out of sight.

Vivian's heart sank as she recognized the source of the commotion—**Evelyn Chase**.

Evelyn was standing with two studio executives, her expression tight with anger, her voice low but fierce. From the few words Vivian could hear, it was clear Evelyn was not happy with how things were unfolding. She wasn't content to stand in the background while Vivian claimed the spotlight.

Vivian's pulse quickened, dread curling in her stomach. She knew Evelyn had powerful connections. And now, seeing her speaking so forcefully with the executives, a fear took hold: Was

Evelyn trying to sabotage her? Was she pulling strings behind the scenes to undermine Vivian's performance, to question the casting choice?

She turned to find Rob at her side, his jaw clenched as he watched the scene unfold. He didn't speak, but his tension was palpable.

"What's happening?" Vivian whispered, her voice tight.

Rob's eyes flicked to hers, dark with concern. "I don't know. But whatever it is, it's not good."

Before Vivian could respond, one of the executives—**Alan Winters**, a powerful producer with a reputation for making or breaking careers—broke away from the group and walked toward them. His expression was calm, but there was a hint of something cold in his eyes as he approached.

"Vivian," Winters said smoothly, his voice polite but distant. "A word?"

Vivian's throat tightened. She could feel the eyes of the crew on her, the weight of the moment pressing down like a suffocating blanket. She glanced at Rob, who gave her a barely perceptible nod of encouragement.

"Yes?" she managed, her voice steady despite the panic rising inside her.

Winters folded his arms, his expression unreadable. "I've been having conversations with some of the studio heads. There are concerns about the direction the film is taking. Concerns about... certain casting decisions."

The words hit her like a punch. *Concerns about casting decisions.* It was clear what that meant. Evelyn was making her move, trying to claw back the role that had slipped through her fingers. And Winters, with his power and influence, was the perfect ally for her.

Vivian's heart raced, but she forced herself to remain calm. She had worked too hard to let this slip away now.

"Is there something specific you're concerned about?" she asked, her voice steady.

Winters hesitated, as if weighing his next words carefully. "Let's just say there's been some discussion about whether you're the right fit for this role. We want to ensure the best possible outcome for the film, and we're not entirely convinced that... well, that we've made the right choice."

The words were like a cold slap, and Vivian felt the ground shift beneath her. After everything—after the audition, the test shoot, the emotion she had poured into the role—was it still not enough? Was Hollywood's game so rigged that even her best wasn't good enough to secure her place?

But before she could respond, Rob stepped forward, his voice firm and resolute.

"Alan," Rob said, his tone laced with barely contained anger, "this isn't about what's best for the film. This is about politics, and you know it. Vivian was chosen because she's the best for the role. And if you'd bothered to watch the scene we just shot, you'd see that."

Winters narrowed his eyes, clearly unaccustomed to being challenged. "This is about more than one scene, Rob. It's about the entire picture. We need—"

"No," Rob interrupted, his voice rising. "What you need is to stop playing these games. Vivian earned this role. You saw what she just did. She's perfect for Sophie, and you know it. Don't let Evelyn's maneuvering cloud your judgment."

Vivian's heart swelled at Rob's words, but fear still gnawed at her. She knew how fragile the balance of power in Hollywood was—how easily someone like Evelyn could tilt the scales.

Winters studied them both for a long moment, his expression hard. Then, with a slight nod, he turned on his heel and walked back toward Evelyn, leaving Vivian and Rob standing alone in the middle of the snow-covered set.

For a long moment, neither of them spoke. The tension in the air was thick, the unspoken threat of what had just transpired hanging over them like a storm cloud.

But then, slowly, the energy shifted. Rob turned to her, his eyes filled with fierce determination. "You're not losing this role, Vivian. Not to them. You deserve this."

Vivian nodded, her heart pounding with a mixture of fear and resolve. She wasn't going to back down. Not now. Not after everything she had been through.

"Come on," Rob said, his voice quiet but firm. "Let's go back to the set. We've got more to shoot."

Vivian took a deep breath, steadying herself. The battle wasn't over, but she wasn't alone in it. With Rob by her side, she felt stronger, more certain.

And as she walked back toward the twinkling lights and the falling snow, she knew one thing for sure:

She wasn't going to let anyone—Evelyn, Winters, or anyone else—take this from her. Not when she had fought so hard to get here.

Not when she had found her voice, her strength, and, for the first time, her true self.

This was her breakthrough, and nothing was going to stop her now.

10
A NEW BEGINNING

The days after the confrontation on set passed in a haze of quiet determination. The storm of Hollywood politics that had threatened to topple everything Vivian had worked for seemed to fade into the background, like the last remnants of a bad dream. She hadn't heard from Evelyn since that tense Christmas Day, and Alan Winters, despite his influence, had retreated into silence after his failed attempt to sway the studio. In the end, the performance had spoken louder than the politics, and Harrington had stood by his decision.

Vivian Gray was officially Sophie. *Holiday in Dreamland* was moving forward with her as the star.

But while the studio may have cast her in the role, the true victory was something much deeper, something more personal. She had fought not just for her place in Hollywood, but for her own sense of self. And as she stood on the set of *Holiday in Dreamland*, looking around at the snow-covered town square where she had filmed that pivotal scene, a quiet realization settled over her: she had made it. Not just in the way that mattered to the tabloids and the producers, but in a way that mattered to her. She had stayed true to herself.

The final day of filming had a bittersweet quality. The entire crew buzzed with the usual energy of wrapping a film, but there was also something more—an unspoken acknowledgement that this wasn't just another movie. There was magic in this project, something intangible that Rob had woven into his script, something that had captured the hearts of everyone involved.

Vivian stood at the edge of the set, watching as the crew dismantled the Christmas decorations and packed away the lights. The set, once so vibrant and full of holiday cheer, was slowly being stripped down to its bones. It was a strange feeling, watching the world of *Holiday in Dreamland* disappear, knowing that soon it would only exist on the screen.

The last scene they'd filmed had been a quiet one. Sophie, standing in the town square as the snow fell around her, realizing that she wasn't alone anymore. The love she had thought lost forever had found her again, not in the form of the man she had mourned, but in the new, unexpected love that had grown in its place. It was a simple, delicate moment—the perfect end to the story. And in many ways, it mirrored what Vivian had been feeling in her own life.

As the crew bustled around her, she felt a presence at her side. She turned to see **Rob Dalton** standing next to her, his hands in his pockets, his expression thoughtful as he watched the set being dismantled.

"It's over," Vivian said softly, though the words carried more weight than she had anticipated.

Rob nodded, his eyes still on the crew. "It is."

They stood in silence for a moment, both of them absorbing the significance of the day. It wasn't just the end of the film—it was the end of a journey that had changed them both.

"You did it," Rob said finally, turning to look at her. "You were incredible, Vivian."

Vivian smiled, though there was a hint of sadness in her expression. "We did it," she corrected. "You wrote the story. You gave it life."

Rob shook his head. "I may have written the words, but you brought Sophie to life in a way I never could have imagined."

There was something unspoken in his words, a depth of emotion that hung in the air between them. For so long, their connection had been tied to the film, to the characters and the story that had drawn them together. But now, with the film completed, there was a quiet question lingering between them: What happens next?

Vivian looked at him, her heart pounding in her chest. "What now, Rob?"

He met her gaze, his eyes filled with the same vulnerability he had shared with her on that night weeks ago, when he had first told her about Clara, about the pain that had shaped him. But now there was something else in his expression—something softer, more hopeful.

"I don't know," he admitted, his voice quiet. "But I know one thing. I don't want this—whatever this is between us—to end with the film."

Vivian's breath caught, and for a moment, she felt the weight of everything that had happened between them. The ups and downs, the uncertainty, the push and pull between ambition and love. She had spent so long questioning whether what they had was real, or if it was just another part of the Hollywood game. But here, now, as they stood on the set where they had poured so much of themselves into the story, she realized that what they had was more than just the product of a film.

It was real.

Vivian reached for his hand, her fingers curling around his, and the tension that had been building inside her for weeks finally melted away. For the first time in a long time, she felt at peace.

"I don't want it to end, either," she said softly.

Rob smiled, a quiet, genuine smile that lit up his entire face. They stood there for a moment, hand in hand, as the crew continued to work around them, the world of *Holiday in Dreamland* slowly being packed away. But the magic of the moment lingered, as if the story they had created together wasn't quite finished yet.

Later that evening, Vivian found herself back at her apartment, the same small place she had lived in before all of this had started. But something about it felt different now. She wasn't the same woman who had stared at herself in the mirror, wondering if she was good enough, wondering if she could survive the ruthless world of Hollywood. She had proven to herself—and to the world—that she could.

The apartment was quiet, save for the soft hum of Christmas music playing on the radio. She had decorated a small tree in the corner, its lights twinkling in the dim room, casting a warm glow over the space. The simplicity of it felt right. After all the glitz and glamour of Hollywood, after all the pressure and ambition, it was the quiet moments that mattered most.

There was a knock at the door, and Vivian's heart skipped a beat. She knew who it was before she even opened it.

Rob stood in the doorway, a modest bouquet of flowers in his hand, his expression warm but uncertain. "I thought I'd stop by," he said softly. "I didn't want to leave things unsaid."

Vivian smiled and stepped aside, letting him in. He set the

flowers down on the table and turned to face her, his eyes searching hers.

"You were right," he said, his voice low. "About Hollywood. About how it can change people. But you didn't let it change you, Vivian. You stayed true to yourself."

Vivian felt a lump rise in her throat. "I almost didn't," she admitted. "There were moments when I thought I had lost myself in all of it. But you... you reminded me of what mattered."

Rob stepped closer, his hand brushing hers. "I think we reminded each other."

They stood in the quiet of the apartment, the soft glow of the Christmas lights wrapping around them like a blanket of warmth. It wasn't the kind of grand, Hollywood ending that people wrote scripts about—there were no flashing lights, no sweeping music, no declarations of love in the rain. But it was real. It was theirs.

Vivian looked up at him, her heart full. "I don't know what's going to happen next," she said, echoing the uncertainty she had felt earlier on set. "But I want to find out. With you."

Rob smiled, his eyes soft with emotion. "I want that, too."

And with that, he leaned down and kissed her, a soft, tender kiss that carried with it all the unspoken promises of a new beginning. It wasn't the end of their story—it was the start of something new, something real, something neither of them had quite expected.

As they stood together, wrapped in the glow of the Christmas lights and the warmth of each other's embrace, Vivian knew that she had finally found what she had been searching for all along. It wasn't fame or fortune or the perfect role. It was love. It was connection. It was the understanding that, no matter what Hollywood threw at her, she was strong enough to face it—because she had found herself, and she had found someone who saw her for who she truly was.

And in the quiet magic of that Christmas night, Vivian Gray realized that this was her real breakthrough.

A new beginning, filled with hope, love, and the promise of everything yet to come.

AFTERWORD

As the cameras stopped rolling and the final scene of *Holiday in Dreamland* wrapped, I couldn't help but reflect on the journey that had brought this story to life. What began as a simple tale of ambition and dreams in 1950s Hollywood blossomed into something much deeper—a story of self-discovery, love, and the price we pay for the lives we choose. For Vivian Gray, the glamorous world of cinema wasn't just a backdrop; it was a battleground, one where her greatest challenge wasn't just to succeed, but to remain true to herself in an industry that often demands otherwise.

But as the story unfolded, it became clear that winning the role wasn't the end of her journey. It was only the beginning.

Hollywood is, after all, a place built on illusion—a world where nothing is ever truly as it seems. Behind the glittering lights and the iconic marquees lies a darker truth, a truth that Vivian only began to glimpse as she stepped into the spotlight. The politics, the power plays, the whispered secrets in the halls of the studio—they haven't gone away. If anything, they're just starting to rear their heads.

Vivian's victory in *Holiday in Dreamland* may have cemented her place as a rising star, but the path ahead is fraught with danger. The pressures of fame, the relentless ambition of those around her, and the ghosts of Hollywood's past continue to loom large in the distance. People like Evelyn Chase, who lost the battle but not the war, are still out there, waiting for their moment to strike again.

And then there's **Rob Dalton.** What started as a tender connection between them has turned into something real, something powerful. But Hollywood has a way of testing even the strongest relationships, of twisting love into something transactional. Can their bond survive the forces working against them—the secrets that have yet to surface, the old wounds that refuse to heal?

Because behind every Hollywood dream, there's a hidden cost. And sometimes, the price isn't revealed until it's too late.

As the world around her begins to shift once more, Vivian will face new challenges, ones far more dangerous than she ever imagined. The shadows of Hollywood's past are closing in, bringing with them whispers of scandal and betrayal that could ruin not just her career, but everything she holds dear.

For the real question remains: **How far is Vivian willing to go to protect what she's earned? And what will she do when the very people she trusts the most begin to show their true colors?**

In Hollywood, there are no second chances. But there are always second acts.

And Vivian Gray's story is far from over.

To be continued...

www.ingramcontent.com/pod-product-compliance
Lightning Source LLC
LaVergne TN
LVHW050025080526
838202LV00069B/6922